Grounding from Within

Grounding from Within

―――∞―――

*Musings on Truth,
Discipline, Detachment,
and Joy*

JMG

Grounding from Within: Musings on Truth, Discipline,
Detachment and Joy

© 2020, JMG
jmg@hipcity.co
Hip City Inc.

ISBN: 978-1-7355593-1-5
Cover and interior design by Tabitha Lahr

All rights reserved. No part of this publication may be reproduced, stored in a retrieval system, stored in a database and / or published in any form or by any means, electronic, mechanical, photocopying, recording or otherwise, without the prior written permission of the publisher. If you enjoyed this book, please encourage your friends to download their own copy from their favorite authorized retailer. Thank you for your support.

Printed in the United States of America

To EB and M Sol

Understand Truth 1

Instill Discipline 29

Practice Detachment 57

Experience Joy 85

Understand Truth

"The only true wisdom is
in knowing you know nothing."
—Socrates

People...

in your life want to support you and see you prosper. Lean into them. So often we put up barriers to our own success by creating stories about what others are thinking. Things like I am a burden or I am not worth it. So you don't use the resources offered. These thoughts are never true, and if they seem to be it's because you have projected them to be. You see what you want to see. You cannot do this alone, nor would you want to. We are all part of the shared experience. Use your community as a springboard for growth. Invest in your surroundings and see how everything begins to expand.

Trauma, ...

as little or large as it is, gets lodged in the body. Address this to alleviate it. If you don't, it will slowly build and build until it affects your mind. It will not come in the form of the past—that is done with—it will come in the form of an uncertain future. You will not be able to pinpoint the reason, but the anxiety will keep you stagnant. Remember, there is nothing wrong with you; the event is just something that happened. With awareness and physical exertion, you can remove its effects from your being. Then the mind can go back to creating and building. Heal the body and watch the mind take flight.

Sometimes...

you are at loss for words. That's OK. Everyone is from time to time. Be kind to yourself and others. We never know all the causes, we only know what happens. And often not even that. If you put your feet on the ground, you may feel the shift. Gradually and slowly we are being broken down. It's the state of play. But the drumbeat of rebirth also keeps going. That is what it does. It does not ask and it does not wallow. It moves beyond space, time, and fear.

Understand . . .

that time will bend if you let it. Once you see everything as it is and not as a projection, the false falls away and there is no rush. There is only now. If you don't zero in on that, you will be lost in a sea of despair and longing. The good news is you always have a choice to stop, breathe, and contemplate the moment. Take it in for all that it's worth. See it for what it is and not what you think it should be. If you do this enough, you will have enough time for everything.

Leave . . .

your self-induced isolation that is keeping you from discovery. Turn your anxiety into a strength and asset. It's all in how you look at life. Ride the wave of the moment by establishing routines and discarding thoughts of the future. Embrace the positivity that will often flow through you once you're aware of it. Do not chase external validation. Seek out situations and circumstances that evoke your internal motivation to achieve.

Just . . .

when you think you have something in place, it changes. You discover that its perceived stability was an illusion. The truth does not waver and will not change. It's here and now. The course you travel on is the destination itself. Remove the false ideas around you as much as possible. This includes attachment to lives not lived. Let go of all of it. It is no use to lament for something that is not there. Instead, find new patterns and ideas through monetary circulation, gratitude, and awareness.

Accept goodness . . .

in all of its forms. As it comes through in your life, recognize it and be grateful for it. Be careful not to self-sabotage. The mind may concoct a story of you not deserving it. It does this to feel a validation for its existence. It is the problem-solver, so often it will create problems so it can appear useful to you. In reality your inner voice that lies beyond the mind paints a real picture. It knows nothing else.

You...

may question your place in the world. That's not up to you to decide. It's only up to you to embrace what will best serve you and others. And trust all is where it should be at the present moment. This peace is around you if you want to access it. You can't read anyone's mind, so what makes you think you can read yours? Half the stuff is just regurgitated totems you have been told to worry about, to fear, and to run from. They may be true or false, but they're all myths if they have not happened yet. So why dwell on them? If they do occur, know you will deal with them and move on.

Opportunity . . .

may lie in unexpected places. What seems like a huge project may not be once you start into it. Go in with an open mind, and worry less about how something is done than the direction it trends. Soon enough what is already being accomplished on your behalf will be apparent. Then you just follow the signs. Move forward, expecting all will go as it should. No more, no less.

It's not...

about you. The causes of an event are too numerous to triangulate, so you always default to thinking it's about you. It's not. Everything has its own cause, and often you will not know what exactly that is. It's OK to not know. To just let things be as they are. Remove your own ideas from the equation and focus only on the truth. Keep mining for reality over and over. You will begin to see it once you disregard everything you thought you knew.

New patterns . . .

are coming up daily. Sit with them. Pay attention to how they move and whether or not items are falling into place around you. If not, ask yourself what is holding them back. Then zero in on the fallacy or the truth at the root of the circumstance. Only through disciplined integration can you begin to understand what can propel you forward. Then you can start focusing on that and let the other stuff drift away.

Your relationships . . .

will be a reflection of your world. If they bring you suffering, they are false. There is nothing to hide and nothing to cover up. Allow others to be heard, but don't let them twist your thoughts or stifle your actions. Focus only on the truth, which is unmistakable and unwavering. Cultivate the relationships that bring you joy and growth and let the others be.

The challenge . . .

for everyone is to cultivate the self that is beyond any label or categorization, that is carrying an energy all of its own. You will not find this self through a bottle or a pill. You will find it only when you give yourself space, and focus on being aware of your actions and reactions. Any rabbit hole you jump down is your own mind's creation, so follow it as far as it takes you—and when you find there is no end to it, ask yourself why you ventured down it in the first place. Why not bypass it altogether and focus on the necessary? Let the illusions and distractions fade away.

Find . . .

the path that works for you. You will know the way when life flows. It will move in waves, with no real direction. Surround yourself with options and ways to be successful. Don't get boxed in by your own false projections. Everything changes, so have a buffer built in to adjust where needed. There are no missed opportunities; there is just what you believe moment to moment. Let go of trying to control every situation. Embrace the unexpected and the movement that occurs naturally.

Authenticity . . .

cannot be proven. If you try to do so, you are bound to fail. It is something that is lived in and that you don't need to waver from or give answers for. People will recognize it when they see it, but it can't be shown to them. You would not want it any other way. It is your core, and what comes from there cannot be stolen, changed, or manipulated. It just is. You can't find something that has never been lost. So stop all the searching, all the plugging, all the manic half-truths, and hero worship. Peace will be the by-product.

Take...

in new ideas and test out new hypotheses each day. Nobody knows the right answer, and each person's reality is different. Let the day be your guide and don't force it. There is no need to dwell. Tread lightly and stay present and aware. The inputs will be constant, so don't let them paralyze you into inactivity. Weave in and out of your mind and put into action what you want to see happen. No more, no less. It's not about the other; it's about you and how you want to live and be. Nobody can take that away from you. You choose.

Slowly uncover . . .

the life you want to lead and go for it. You may have a path that puzzles some, but trust that it will work for you. The signs do not lie. You don't have to cover up truths from yourself. Learn to be alone. Let yourself recharge away from everything. Be accountable to what moves you, and not what you think you should be moved by. Step into the current and see what happens.

The side hustle . . .

is the real one. Don't kid yourself. It's what is in your heart to do, so go do it. Abandon all thoughts and reservations of the contrary and move all in. Trust that it will all work out. You are not what you think you are and never were. Your capabilities are beyond what you believe. If you're going to gamble, it might as well be on yourself. If you do, others will step in to help you along. The payoff is worth it.

So much . . .

of your life is out of your control. That is why it is so important to use your agency when you can. Simply flow to the next action point and engage. If you think about what you 'should' do but you don't do it, you will think you have failed yourself. Beware of the 'shoulds'. It's do or don't do, and that is all it is. In each moment this could change, but as long as you take stock of what is up for you to handle in the present, you can do no wrong. And sometimes that is sitting still.

Be . . .

present and aware of your surroundings. Create to create. Capture and resonate. Forgo compliance at every turn to shatter ceilings. Breathe life into stagnation and dream through darkness. Escape to re-energize. Act to re-establish. Awaken and be counted. Rise in formation and tolerate success. Stop wishing something else was there. Uncover who you are by testing what you aren't. Don't be afraid of what is discovered. Be sure to rest when you're tired, and party when you're awake.

Insanity . . .

is doing the same thing over and over again and expecting a different result. We have all heard of this saying, but we all fall into this behavior from time to time. Don't stress yourself about this. It's a natural impulse. Instead of doing the same thing, choose a different path to find a variant, successful outcome. The simple fact is we don't know what will happen until we act.

You don't know . . .

what you don't know. And that is OK. You may think you do, but oftentimes that is just happenstance. The only way to find out is to venture forth with no expectations. Be sure to plan all you want, but realize it is fool's gold to forecast the result. Life does not take place in a vacuum. Everything and nothing are happening at once. Awareness of this will allow you to feel confident in your direction.

Sweat...

can provide mental, spiritual, and physical healing. It's used as a way to wring out the toxins that inevitably build up in our day-to-day lives. Although you're constantly sweating, you just don't notice it because the cells absorb the liquid before it surfaces on the skin. However, in high sweat production situations such as exercise, physical labor, or heat, the cells don't have the time to reabsorb it. So excess chemicals have a chance to leave the body, which can then re-balance. Harmony in life reflects this internal unison of the body, so you will feel good when sweat has a chance to escape and recalibrate. As in everything else, pay attention and replenish your body as needed. You will be rewarded.

So many . . .

things are working in the background to your advantage. If you sit back and think about where you are and how you got there, you will be overwhelmed by all the occurrences that seemingly fell in place for you. Embrace this thought over and over, for there is more truth in this than anything else. Override all others to the contrary. So many inputs you receive consciously and subconsciously will tell you that you are not enough or are lacking something. That is easily proven false over and over by attention to the moment.

The voices . . .

in your head. Where do they come from and which do you listen to? The first step is to be aware of them. The second step is to investigate them to identify where they may be coming from. The third step is accepting them. The fourth step is moving through them. The fifth step is taking action on the ones that won't go away. Especially the loud, pushy ones that are constantly self-justifying a condition they want to see. Oftentimes this is a misdirected attempt to help that does not do so in the long run. So quiet them with some type of mediation and relaxation. From there will emerge some quieter voices. These are something to ponder and sit with. They come from a different place than your experiences and your knowledge. You will be motivated to learn and grow with them until you transmute them into ideas that serve you and others.

Instill Discipline

"Every step is on the path."
—Lao Tzu

You can . . .

choose whether to be affected by something or not. It happened, but you can choose how you want to respond to it. Sometimes you need to realize others' agendas are not the same as your own. Your frame is your frame of reference. Their frame is based on their own worries and anxiety. The person we think we are is limited and exists only in perception. You can break through this by stepping outside yourself and looking in.

Choose . . .

your own adventure. Again and again. It's up to you to find a lane you can flourish in so that others can witness that it's not a struggle. Spend your life investigating what moves you and what does not. There is no judgment, just curiosity and dedication to the task at hand. Then you let everything flow to you as it seems fit. Through trial and error, you will begin to uncover what you like doing and what you do not. Build a life around this test, and you will be fulfilled and grateful.

There is . . .

a time in your life to do what's best for you. You tap into what you truly want and proceed with abandon. Too often we wait. But the opportunity is here and now. It's yours for the taking. The anxiety comes from your indecision. As soon as you choose, you are on your way. The universe will bend toward your aims, but you are in charge of making the choice to move toward your goals. The how is not up to you. The trust and faith and action are.

Why . . .

is it so hard to ask for help? Why do you think you are weak to do so? Because you think you're not worth it? Because you are ashamed? Because that's what you have been told by your mind? It's nonsense, and you know that in your heart. Your mind thinks it can survive by itself, but it can't. We are constructed to step up. We are designed to help. It's how we have evolved. So not asking for help is counterproductive in two ways. The first, it hurts you because you need help, even if you say you don't. The second, it hurts the person who could be growing by helping you. So get out of your head and ask for help. Then ask again. It's a win-win.

Observe . . .

the topics you discuss which animate you, as well as the ones that don't. Take note of what you are saying and how you are saying it. More importantly, note the energy it brings to you and others. This is a map to what motivates you and how you can help solve problems. Begin building a life around that, and the idea that it is 'work' will be secondary. Don't worry about what you want to do. Instead focus on what provides you natural energy and go from there.

Freedom is . . .

in self-discipline. When you instill this and show up, you'll gain a sense of peace and accomplishment. Set your parameters, follow them, and see what happens. Don't attach yourself to the result either way. The set-up and follow-through are what is important. Let the rest go. You can't control anything but how you respond. Practice this over and over until it becomes secondhand.

Each day . . .

you have a chance at bringing additional light into your orbit. If it does not happen, don't worry about it. Just keep looking for the light. You will always have other chances. You can't force things. To fight against events will lead to frustration and second-guessing. Learn the process of trusting your instincts by witnessing your surroundings at all times. Then let life flow around you as you ride alongside it.

To lash...

out against yourself is counter-productive. You are just promoting suffering from within. You don't have to make that choice. You don't have to allow yourself to succumb to pain from disappointment. Instead, turn the outcome around and see what you can learn from it. You put yourself in this position, so now embrace the challenge of the moment instead of dwelling on the perceived failure in the past.

You are . . .

constantly being inundated with advertising indicating you are not enough. This is false. Realize that through discipline and focus you can live the life you want to live. Be authentic and free. Set up conditions for a sensible and simple life and watch how expansive it becomes.

We all need . . .

routines. They settle the mind and allow you to fall easier and easier into a flow state. They help you establish benchmarks and small victories that you can continue to build on. It is important to take the time to find out what works for you. Build your routines to move naturally along with your day. Practice them with diligence, awareness, and discipline. Set them up to succeed. As you do, check in with yourself on how you may need to augment them in order to keep learning and growing. The progress will show up on its own, as a by-product of orchestrated chaos.

Be aware . . .

of where your ego may be taking you. Most things are out of your control. You are nothing of consequence but entirely essential. It's not about you or your ideas. Stay present and light. Recognize that your truth is subjective to others. And vice versa. Experience weighs in, but only after the fact. So don't take yourself so seriously. Pursue excellence and clarity of vision whenever possible. Keep the slate clean and don't fill your day with wasted motion.

You're 'it' . . .

Nobody else is going to live your life. You have it all in your sights, so proceed. Trust in the signs and venture forth to catch it. If you don't, you will just be kicking yourself later on. Don't buy into the pretense that someone else knows the answer for you. Come up with your plan, put it in place, and don't be afraid to fail. If you do this, outside help will come to you, and you will be able to recognize it when it does. You will not be grasping at anything, but allowing things to happen in the direction that you have intended.

The stuff...

that keeps you up at night rarely comes to pass. They are self-created projections based on past experience, or lack of experience, and they're nothing really to worry about because they're counter-productive. Your mind is trying to prepare you, but what you are undertaking will be learned in the flow, not planned out in your head. If you don't make trivial matters important, they will cease to be important. Pay attention to the direction in which items are moving, instead of wishing something else were there.

Tap in . . .

and grab it. Nobody is going to tell you how, so jump in. Trust your instincts and don't look back. Have fun with it. Bring out the joy in others and it will circle back to you tenfold. It's how it works, so embrace it and roll with it. You choose your reaction to destiny. Move beyond the normal back-and-forth. Pick your spot and deliver with pure thought and straightforwardness. Do not expect knowing to happen; just know it will happen.

Play . . .

the long game. Understand nothing happens overnight. The real stuff is put together step by step until the whole emerges almost despite you. Failure is built in to it, as you continue to tweak until all components are firing on all cylinders. The journey is the destination. If you embrace that, it's all good. So put in the time but only if it's freedom to you, not work. Mentally set yourself up, telling yourself you have already won, and you will have. Everyone can determine what that means for themselves, but others can't for you.

Create lanes . . .

of space in your day wherever you can. Then see what fills them up. As you go along, eliminate what does not serve you and you will find you have more room than you thought. Don't worry about the be all and end all. Focus on the day to day. More and more of your life will be fulfilling and resonant. That's what we're all seeking: a life full of balance and possibility, becoming re-born by the moment.

If you . . .

keep devoted to something you love to do, you will improve. Progress may not be measurable on a day-to-day basis, which can seem stagnant. But it's not. Each day you learn more and more about the approaches that fit your personality. There is no one way to accomplish things. The possibilities are endless. But if you keep learning and growing, you'll get where you want to go. There are no shortcuts. And that's why the progress is memorable.

Recognize . . .

the difference between activity and action. Action is intention, and it transforms. Activity is movement, and it placates. Your heart wants action. Your mind can drown in activity. Focus on what you want to see happen and then take the steps to get it done. Don't do things just for motion's sake. Find and uncover the motive, or let it go.

Every day . . .

everything changes and nothing does. It's all in how you look at it. We are all just figuring it out, one step at a time. Some days the steps are there for you to access; other days they seem hidden. In those days it is important to not panic or be fearful. Realize the steps are still there; you just can't see them at this moment. This will pass. If you stay focused on the truth and patient with your vision, you will be shown the way forward.

Go forward...

with a path in mind and let it play out. Take it step by step and day by day. Nudging a little farther along as you go. As your mind wanders to bigger and better things, go back to the task at hand and finish it. After doing this over and over, you will begin to see the results emerge. Embrace the little accomplishments and move forward with the next in line.

To doubt . . .

is natural. It's how we are wired, but you don't have to buy into it. Remove your identity from the equation. In the end it does not matter who people think you are. It's in their heads and their heads alone. Remember, their experiences are what will form their opinion of you. And you have little control over that. All you do have is your own dedicated agency. So use it. Take your time and settle in. Too often we are covering something up and not letting it breathe.

Be aware . . .

and diligent of checking in . . . with your health, wealth, and purpose. With so many different channels overwhelming our circuits daily, it's important to take stock from time to time on the direction you're headed, and whether you want to continue down that path. There are countless ways to do this, but you have to figure out the best way for you. When you do, your truth will emerge from the shadows. But it will not appear to you if you never check in. As you do, you will gain more and more confidence in what feels correct to you, while releasing what does not. It will be a feeling of peace and certainty that will be undeniable.

Each . . .

of us has our own concerns and assumptions that will surface when we're vulnerable, and that's natural. Realize these are your perceptions and nobody else's. So you can make the choice to not be controlled by them. Tell your story the truest way you know how and then let go of the outcome. Keep putting it out there without expecting anything in return. Some people will want you to change because it fits their impression better. Or serves their agenda. Accept this as their understanding, but don't let it bleed into your own if it does not serve you. Stand tall and do the work. Deflect the shots as they come up.

Get back at it . . .

Learn from your mistakes and take the challenge again and again. Each time you do you will only be closer and closer to your end goal. It's short, choppy steps but they add up in the long run. Others may see this as magic, but it's not so. Everyone has this capacity if they choose to do so, because anyone can author their own reality. Just do it a couple of times. You will be surprised how often things fall into place.

Move . . .

against tendency and set a new pattern to see what emerges. Our experience seems to predicate the next move, but oftentimes this is false information. We are wired to think we know the future, but we really have little control of how something is going to proceed. The control we do have is to recognize we don't have it. So where does this put us? What inner voices are best to tap into? One way is to be focused and aware of who is saying what and to whom.

Practice Detachment

"The root of suffering is attachment."
—GAUTAMA BUDDHA

Stay . . .

out of your own way. Things happen from all kinds of circumstances, none and all of which are related to you. Your job is to be with them. Don't run away and don't chase. Don't reason with and don't grasp. Just embrace them all fully. Sometimes you will think it is hard, and sometimes you will think it's easy. The important thing is to keep full awareness of what is really going on and not what your mind is jumping to conclusions on. It's a fine line, but one worth treading. When you do, you will find that no matter what is going on around you, a sense of calm and peace will preside because you are detached but present.

You will . . .

fail over and over. Accept this fact and realize everyone does. You fail because you are trying. You're trying to temper suffering, you're trying to make yourself and loved ones happy. You soon recognize the folly in trying to mold something that can't be molded. There is only action and timing. Let go of things out of your control.

Follow . . .

your natural instinct. Trust it to take you to where you eventually want to go. It is OK that it takes a different route than you imagined. That's all part of the process. Mentally stake a claim and let go of the how. Focus on the why and the connection. Move with continuance and clarity. Lead with directness, earnestness, and compassion.

If...

you see something in your life or in your thoughts as static, it is an illusion. It does not exist. Look around you. Everything evolves. To fight against that is a fool's game. You are fighting for changeless outcomes, which will never happen. Such scenarios exist only in our minds. When you find yourself in the narrative of certainty and absolutes, take a step back and look at all the pieces in motion. There are many which you don't see, and all of them transform.

When things . . .

are in divine timing, they fall into place naturally. There seems to be no effort made or issue weighed. It just is what it is. There is no better and there is no worse. There is no success and there is no failure. Creation is the beat that drums, and progress goes along for the ride. For this to happen in your endeavors, let go of outward control. Be hyper-aware when the pieces are in place, and go forward without fear or anxiety.

You're constantly . . .

surrounded by chaos and change. Different thoughts, different situations, different results seem to come from everywhere and nowhere. So how does one remain focused and steady? The only way is to move with it, but not in it. This means not attaching any personal opinion or judgment as it swirls around you, and not letting it stop you from doing what needs to be done.

When you're . . .

at an impasse, sometimes it's best to stop and be still. You're in the way of something that needs to happen. Instead of denying it, do your part and remove your mind and body from the premises. Just sit with the issue on the sidelines. Soon enough it may resolve. If it doesn't, it did not hurt to be still. Too often we think we need to do something, when in actuality it's the opposite. Just doing nothing and being present for a bit and letting a situation breathe is often the sane course of action. And may get you the results you desire.

The mind . . .

is a curious instrument. Examine it, but don't try to explain it. Drill down on why certain thoughts come up. Do they hurt or help? What programming has created them for you? Realize you can displace the harmful ones with others that help you live a more in-tune lifestyle. Change your mode from grasping to appreciation. Let go of expectations. Walk the clean path and embrace integrity.

You know . . .

when you're in it. Everything falls into place. There is no effort, just action. You remain anchored to the present and let the past and future go. You think of something and it appears. You send out love and it comes back in return. Everything seems to be dreamlike, almost too good to be true, but it's not. It is our most balanced and true emotional state. You're not grasping for anything or searching for other options or answers. You don't over-analyze; you move with fluidity, purpose, and grace. You know that in the end you contain all of what you need.

The future...

can sometimes seem too blinding to face. Too overwhelming, too circumspect, too rigid, too opaque, too sad, too joyful, too hopeful to get your mind around. So it waits, looming. It can be a struggle to put one foot in front of the other. Leave the moment of despair when it appears, for it's not real. It's an imaginative amalgamation, a type of string theory that misses the mark. You have everything you need. It is a matter of getting out of your own way. Follow these three little steps: observe, act if needed, and detach.

Time . . .

does not exist. You only think it does by tracking and categorizing it. But in reality, or in the present moment, nothing is lost and nothing is gained. It just is. It is your mind that leaps forward or looks back in an attempt make sense of things. Don't attach yourself to this, for this is what the mind does. The only reality that exists is what is right in front of you. Embrace and pay attention to that, and all your anxiety will fade away.

Look . . .

for counterbalance in each situation. If something goes up, it will come down. Sometimes it seems that the deck is stacked against you, but that's a false front. Opportunity is everywhere; accept it. Which is harder than it looks. But don't let it be. Go with the flow—if it bends, you bend. There is hardly any reason to go against it. Except your mind telling you that you have to. When you let go of the resistance, the situation is flipped on its head. And as soon as it goes one way, it can just as easily go the other. Don't let a small setback turn into an avalanche.

You cannot . . .

alleviate someone's suffering. You can set up conditions to lessen it, but they will have to do it themselves. Nothing you can say will comfort them until they are ready for it. It is not your place to direct, so don't let their anxiety seep into you. Be present and acknowledge the feelings, but be detached from them in your spirit and your outlook. Don't let outside forces pull you under. They cannot touch you if you don't want them to. Move beyond both pain and pleasure to find a calming state of acceptance.

The path . . .

forward is not always seen. Sometimes you have to proceed blindly before your footing begins to take hold. Too often we think one way and find another staring us down. You can make all the plans you want, but be open to change. It's coming for you either way. Trust in the fundamentals and never let go of the big picture. The future will be here soon enough, and then you can partake. Until then, let go of the worry and the predictions.

Accept...

the changes that are out of your control, and let resistance to them go. If you don't, you will continue to obsess about the past until it magnifies more and more. If you remove yourself from the result, it no longer weighs on you, and you can figure out the best solution going forward. There is always a workaround. Trust in your ability to find it. The first step is releasing expectations.

Don't get attached . . .

to time. Give it away and watch it come back to you in more ways than you can imagine. Do not be a prisoner to it. Do not horde it. Do not fight for it. All we have is time, and it is always plentiful, unless you approach it from the sense of control and desperation. Then it will seem you can never have enough. But if you don't get attached to it, it will not concern you. Concentrate on doing useful and joyful things with your time, and it will seem to expand.

Prepare . . .

the best you can and then let go of the worry. Be kind to yourself and open to natural change. Take matters day by day, and give yourself the benefit of the doubt. Other people may think they know the best for you, but remember that their judgments are from their prism of life, not yours. If you think that their unsolicited advice is from a negative filter, you don't have to pay attention to it. The truth in any situation will reveal itself in time.

Let go . . .

of the needless fear of the unknown. Change is coming whether you like it or not. Evolution and re-birth never stop. Each day we have an opportunity to let the metamorphosis sink in more and more. You don't have to chase anything, because transition will arrive soon enough. Accept and flow with these developments as much as you can. Then act to align and surround yourself with the shift. As always, the path is for you to experience, and it will move with you if you let it.

When you . . .

sense a big change in your circumstances, you will begin to look for ways to control it. Your ego will be scared of losing something. Watch your reaction and detach from the fear it conjures. Recognize that change is inevitable, but suffering from the unknown does not have to go with it. Once you realize this, you can begin to manage your reaction to change. With this will come acceptance and new opportunities.

Fear-based...

delusions. They seem to be everywhere and nowhere. All of them are imagined and never experienced. Even if the very thing you thought would occur did, you would not recognize or feel it as you thought you would. For the real is unnoticed, and overridden second by second. Nothing you can imagine will be exactly like you think. That is why the labels we use will keep us in quicksand and flailing. Unburden yourself from them. They don't define you.

Plans . . .

seem to place unnecessary burdens on our psyche. Why do we stress over them? Expectations begin to arise and emotions are tied to them long before they even are supposed to occur. It leaves you with a sense of being pinned in, instead of flowing with them. Allow spontaneity in your life. Let go of the fear of the unknown. It does not have to control you. Make all the plans you want but as soon as they're made, disconnect from them. Use them as a guide but, don't get attached to the results. It all works out.

Often . . .

we can't understand what's really going on. We think we know something until we don't. Then it's time to re-arrange. Don't get attached to one way of thinking or doing. For it will all change and you will think you've been left behind. Instead, be nimble and open-minded. Expect the best and accept all that passes through you. Allow it to flow instead of putting a cap on it. This way you will begin to gain autonomy over it. You will learn that although you control very little that happens, you can control your reaction to all of it.

Sometimes . . .

you have to go back to the basics to re-learn a skill. Or attempt something new. Embrace the starting point. You are a beginner again, with great leaps in front of you. Stay present and release the past. Be grateful that it took you to this point, but it's time to go to another level. The only way to move forward is to let go and move through the moment. Again and again. After some time, the struggle fades away and is replaced by confidence and awareness of the new paradigm.

When situations . . .

are not aligning for you, take a deep breath and reformulate the plan. Or the plan that you think will happen, even though you're not sure it will. You still have your agency and your direction. No matter what actually occurs. Eliminate the noise and focus in to reflect out what you want to see. Oftentimes this resides in switching the momentum for a bit. You have removed yourself from the result, so peace will eventually appear. The side product is the action itself.

Don't . . .

let your emotions dictate your full reaction. Recognize that they exist, but don't bow to them. If you do, you may compound the problem. Pride and ego are camouflaged as protection, but really they will just bring you suffering. Sit with them and let them be, but don't react. Be a witness to this and watch it happen, beyond your control. Because your reaction and your desire are never enough. Each second everything changes. Like a wave crashing into the water, it all dissolves into the source itself. Don't let the drama continue to play out in your mind. It will just build and build unnecessarily, until it's something that never existed in the first place.

Experience Joy

"Being happy, making happy is the rhythm of life."
—Sri Nisargadatta Maharaj

A superpower . . .

is at your disposal. It involves one mantra that you repeat in your mind. Whatever is going on around you, either painful or joyful, simply repeat the phrase *I accept this moment*. Over and over again. Do it for yourself. You will find that joy is heightened and pain lessened. Suffering is caused by fighting or wishing against the moment. When you accept the moment, suffering will vanish. After you accept one moment, you will be on to the next one. You then realize you are free. Repeat as often as you can throughout the day, and you'll begin to find everything will flow.

Life is . . .

not hard. When it seems that way, realize that too much control, too much worry, too much fear have been manifested in your mind. What is the way out? Go to a physical space that brings you joy. A place that takes you out of your head and into heartfelt appreciation and gratitude. Let go of the control you think you have, and appreciate the moment.

The search . . .

is over, and it's just begun. Realize the futility in trying to imagine how you will feel in the future. You can't find something you never lost in the first place. You're not missing anything; you just think you are. The path forward lies in re-discovering your bliss. It's easy if you accept setbacks. Ignore the voices in your head that tell you different. Embrace the voices in your head that tell you you will overcome. The situation is always fluid, so if you ride the waves instead of fighting them, it will be much smoother.

The long days . . .

will get shorter. The choices you make reflect your disposition. So be humble and be present. From there watch as your world shows up to support you. Don't wallow in suffering and disenchantment. It's not what you are built for. We're dynamic, limitless, and transcendental. Accept it. Then model it.

This persona . . .

you have built up is false. Accept it for what it is. It is created only from memories and from habits. It's not your fault. It is a system your mind builds for you to achieve some importance. But it's all fleeting and unnecessary. Cast off all the moorings that are keeping you in this box you think you need to be in to feel safe. Pursue what truly brings you joy. Things you would do for nothing. Things that ring true to you. Things you can't put a price tag on. Don't spend your time watching amalgamations of other people's dreams paraded in front of you. Spend time pursuing truth in whatever avenue speaks to you. Over and over and over again. You will know when your truth takes over your body and soul. Run with it. Trust you will be supported, and you will. You are the consciousness of the moment. You are the creator of it, so you can do whatever is necessary to keep the momentum going.

Awareness . . .

harnesses the energy that reveals truth that lies in plain sight. Through trial and error and repetition and experience, barriers will begin to recede and light will emerge. Trust your path as it begins to show itself through various signposts. Learn to recognize patterns in your mind's thoughts and then release them. From there the elements of change will begin to form, then solidify.

If something speaks . . .

to you, then go be it. You don't have to seek permission from yourself or outside influences. All you have to do is zero in on and pursue what makes your soul happy. This is not to be confused with your body or mind being happy. It is more a focus on your timeless being, something from your first memories you have wanted or have been drawn to. Realize that no outside influence will fill the void, so understand it's here and now. You may as well as pursue your muse on whatever level you can. Focus in on 'the way', not the objective. That will change as you move along. There are no timetables, limits, or terms. Spend time discovering it.

Opportunity...

may lie in unexpected places. What seems like a huge project may not be once you start into it. Go in with an open mind, and worry less about how something is done than the direction it trends. Soon enough what is already being accomplished on your behalf will be apparent. Then you just follow the signs. Move forward, expecting all will go as it should. No more, no less.

Don't over-complicate . . .

the problem because your ego is telling you to do so. Don't be scared of change or run from it. Don't let stress drive your actions. Set your intention and let go. Let go of expectations, let go of fear, let go of pain and suffering. Let go of seriousness, let go of the voices permeating your mind, let go of control, let go of analysis, and let go of the results. Enjoy the moment for what it is, and enjoy the freedom you have when you recognize it.

New ideas and new life . . .

will always bubble up if you make room for them. Cast off the old ways of doing things if they don't serve you any longer. Take stock of what is important, then move past the rest. The era of just grinding away without thought or purpose is over. You are now challenged to help and to provide for others. If you do, your life will change. Your frame for existence will change. You will be more aligned with what matters, and you will be rewarded for it. In ways that you can only imagine.

You cannot . . .

help but gain more and more perspective as you grow. You begin to see the whole picture and focus less on the grind in the blocking and tackling of the day. You feel a sense of peace, as you no longer seek to chase anything. You realize that everything is arriving with purpose. You pay attention to where your mind goes and how you react to events. Keep taking the small steps to experience gratitude, joy, and the pursuit of what you believe you are born to do. Keep building each day where you want to be and release all "knowledge" of how it's supposed to happen. Show up for the ride.

Constant fear . . .

and doubt can infect the mind and poison the soul. Don't let them. Rise above platitudes and illusions of control. The only thing for certain is uncertainty. Take the next step that's in front of you. Little by little you build up and tear down simultaneously. Soon you will find yourself creating what you want to see, and living in the ever-changing present. You will calmly flow in and out of what you seek to accomplish, and experience the richness of the flashing moment. This seems to be a simple truth.

Honor yourself, . . .

and others will follow. Reject yourself and live with the consequences. The soft voices do not lie; you only sometimes think they do. See life through a new prism. See it through a spectrum of joy and suffering. Be aware of the emotion that fits your moment, and then move through it. Sometimes abandoning all you have compiled is the way to find a new outlet. Your creativity will not stop. As a new path takes shape, walk it to see what transpires.

You control . . .

your attention to your thoughts. You and you alone. So filter and embrace the positive ones when they pass through. Let go of the negative ones that have not happened. Do this every day so it becomes your thought pattern. Trust it and practice it until it becomes second nature. Over and over again. Soon you will be redirecting your mind. The negative thoughts will become a slight mummer off in the distance, and the positive ones will become a beautiful choir front and center.

Enter . . .

the new phase light on your feet and with anticipation and gratitude. The moment has brought you here, so now embrace the new challenge ahead. All the circumstances and experiences have led to this new undertaking. The resources will come to you to complete it, because they always do. Trust in the spirit and the excitement of the moment, and bring all of your passion, positivity, and expertise to the forefront. This new phase will unfold as it needs to, and you will be happily along for the ride. In a sense it's already here. It just has not appeared in your plane of sight yet.

Stay present . . .

and follow your joy. Do not judge it, do not seek anything other than it. Cultivate it. Live in it. As you embrace this in yourself, it will be sent outward to others. They will pick up on this energy and roll it into their own manifestation. Over and over again the energy will repeat and expand, helping out everyone involved. Give it a go and see what happens.

Lasting change . . .

moves slowly. By nature it must, in order to really sink in. It's around you when you don't see it and slowly creeps into everyone's consciousness. It's evolution, and despite what you hear it's happening every day. Every day we experience an end and a new beginning. Your mind will begin to accept it as you test it for yourself. Lasting change is in connection, it's in gratitude, it's in compassion, and it's in your family. Mine it there and let it expand outward. So go ahead, tap in, and see for yourself. Your world is waiting for you.

Don't over-complicate...

things. Serve and see what happens. Do focus on what you want to accomplish but do not worry about the steps it will take to get there. Just do the work when it is presented to you, and it will all add up. Too often we get caught up in what may happen, instead of embracing the fact that it is already happening. When you get to this space, your world opens up and happiness becomes the by-product.

What is . . .

the true freedom that you seek to attain? Can it be as simple as accepting what is in front of you at the moment? Chase what you want to chase, but understand that at the end of the day it may not matter. The only thing that does matter is how you let go and give. This does not mean you are passive; instead you are active in the arena you choose to enter. And you're grateful for the fulfillment that comes your way.

Walk the earth...

until it's a hell yes. It's as simple as it sounds. Follow your curiosity and be open to opportunities as they present themselves. Don't be afraid of temporary discomfort if you are working toward an end that you believe in with your whole heart. But if you don't, leave that path until you do. Or never pursue it. Be true to yourself before you help others. Take as much or as little time as you need. There is no such thing as missing out.

We are . . .

all connected, for good or bad. Why not aim for better, instead of worse? They are two sides to everything. One side is joy, the other is suffering. Both start with words and filter down to actions. We experience both sides. The side you focus on is up to you and will reflect your life. The choice is up to you. If you choose suffering, you will perceive your world as cruel, unfair, divided, full of fear and longing. If you choose joy, you will perceive your world as accepting, open, just, and full of freedom and opportunity. A sage once said, 'Make happy, be happy.'

Realize . . .

all things that come to you by external validation are fleeting. Don't put any more or less weight on them. They exist, and that's enough. No need to justify or decry them. Keep focused on the next step and move toward it with confidence and clarity. Use your mind as a tool, not the final verdict. Clean, clear, and contained toward your larger mission. Your heart can free you if you let it. If you lead more with it, most struggles will seemingly melt away. Pass this knowledge to others and watch what happens to them.

We are all . . .

one until we aren't. Separation and comparison are the root of suffering in everyone. We have apps designed to accentuate this, and industries created to prey on our perceived differences and exclusions. Don't succumb to them. Labels are all part of your imagination and false. Move beyond the simple math. The truth lies in the unmanifested that is waiting to break through in all of us. There is no outside rank to achieve or position to chase. You just think there is. Shatter that and you will have a chance to be fulfilled.

Don't live . . .

in the past, but appreciate it. Imagine what you were feeling and possibly fearing, and then look where you are today. It never even existed but, it propelled you to your current space. So honor the memory but do not fixate on it. Bring awareness to the moments and what it took, and did not take, to sit where you sit now. Realize it has no bearing on your future unless you want it to. It's what makes us unique, this ability to gaze backward for brief moments of reflection. Use it as a tool, not a crutch. Promote the joy.

Less thinking . . .

and less doing what you think you should do because others are doing it. Less sitting around in your head. Less forced preparation. Less work. Less struggle. Fewer expectations. Less pressure. Less control. Less fear. More in the flow. More movement. More joy. More spontaneity. More creativity. More bliss. More awe. More happiness. More peace. More appreciation. More gratitude. More love. More light. More awareness. More acceptance.

We all have a boundless capacity to navigate change. We are built to adapt and thrive. Trust your acute inner knowing and cultivate steady growth. Thank you for reading Grounding from Within. *All the best.*

—JMG

www.ingramcontent.com/pod-product-compliance
Lightning Source LLC
Chambersburg PA
CBHW020541080526
44583CB00013B/935